Believe God
for
SOMETHING
BIG

LINDA LEE WHITE

WestBow
PRESS
A DIVISION OF THOMAS NELSON

WestBow Press books may be ordered through booksellers or by contacting:

WestBow Press
A Division of Thomas Nelson
1663 Liberty Drive
Bloomington, IN 47403
www.westbowpress.com
1-(866) 928-1240

Because of the dynamic nature of the Internet, any web addresses or links contained in this book may have changed since publication and may no longer be valid. The views expressed in this work are solely those of the author and do not necessarily reflect the views of the publisher, and the publisher hereby disclaims any responsibility for them.

Any people depicted in stock imagery provided by Thinkstock are models, and such images are being used for illustrative purposes only.

Certain stock imagery © Thinkstock.

ISBN: 978-1-4497-6758-7 (e)
ISBN: 978-1-4497-6757-0 (sc)

Library of Congress Control Number: 2012916958

Unless otherwise noted, all Scripture references in this book are taken from the New King James Version®, copyright © 1982 by Thomas Nelson, Inc. Used by permission. All rights reserved.

Printed in the United States of America

WestBow Press rev. date: 10/9/2012

For My Mom and Dad

Contents

Foreword
By Dan Darr

My name is Dan Darr, and I personally know Linda Lee White to be a most sincere and loving person. She and I became acquainted when my wife and I moved from Dallas, Texas, to Pickerington, Ohio. We rented a cabin on Linda's property. To date (and next to my wife) I have never met a more caring and compassionate person, who exemplifies in every way a *real Christian*. In the six years that we lived by Linda Lee, we had many opportunities to engage in long talks about life and about the goodness of God. I know firsthand that the writings in this book are true, as we have discussed many of the miracles that Linda Lee has referenced in this book.

Believe God for Something Big will increase your faith like nothing else. The reports in this book will increase your conviction and make it possible for you to be able to believe God for the impossible! In these turbulent times, when it seems the entire world is upside down, we need a word that we can hold to, something that will increase our expectancy in God to be able to believe for the absolute impossible and see God move in our behalf. The one thread that runs through this book is the fact that God specializes in *impossibilities*. You will see for yourself how one family's tests and trials have always ended in triumphant victory! Linda Lee explains in detail the attacks that she and her family have had to face, but she also shows you how to continue to believe God no matter what. The story of the deer is just one example of her tenacity in the Spirit. She and her friend did not take *no* for an answer. As it turns out, that miracle opened the door for Linda Lee to minister to the man and his son. God in action … at the right time and the right place.

As you go through the first chapter and on to the second and third, you will find yourself unable to put down this book. You will definitely connect with the author, because her style is as pure and real as it gets, and you will find yourself identifying with many of the impossible situations cited. After I read this book, I found myself remembering the many situations that I have found myself in and remembering the victories I have had in my life over the years. It opened up all those feelings of triumph and success and renewed in me hope for any test that may come down the pike in the future. This book is so worth your time. It will build your faith in God—and no one can tell it quite like Linda Lee—simple, yet profound! May God bless you in the same way as you read *Believe God for Something Big.*

Dan Darr is Care Pastor at a local church, Care Provider to the Impaired, and a retired AT&T manager.

Introduction

I was rushing out the door to get in my car and drive to work. I am like the old cartoon character, Dagwood Bumstead, when it comes to leaving the house. I rush about frantically and then burst out the door in a mad dash. It's really quite crazy.

This particular morning, while racing to the car, I got a little too close to the protruding license plate. It slit my pants and cut my leg with a painful gash. The next day, while babysitting my three-year-old nephew, Jeremiah, I sat on a chair and removed the bandage from my leg. When he saw the jagged cut, he came closer and pointed to my leg, saying, "Owie." I explained what happened, and he was moved with compassion. He swiftly put his little hand over the cut and bowed his head, saying simply, "Jesus heal *Winda Wee*." When he opened his eyes and removed his hand, he looked up at me with astonishment and said, "But, it's still there!" I'll never forget the look on his face. He was totally shocked that the cut was still there. I would have been totally shocked if the cut *wasn't* there! This child was so completely convinced that God's Word was true that he couldn't believe his eyes! At that moment I saw what faith really looks like and sounds like. I also realized I had a long way to go in order to have that kind of childlike faith.

My personal version of faith at that point was that it would just heal fast, and it *did* heal quickly with no scars. But, I realized I needed to believe God for something big ... something mind boggling ... something that would bring God great glory! God loves to do great things that cause encouragement in everyone involved—a building of faith and individual walks with God. God looks for opportunities to prove that every Word He has written is true and that the power He has given us is real.

In today's age we have many fierce enemies that threaten our very lives. There are ravenous diseases like cancer, diabetes, and heart disease. There are enemies that specifically attack our children, like autism, pedophilia, kidnapping, drug addiction, and slavery. We have enemies that want us to live in fear every day of sudden disaster like terrorism or financial collapse. These enemies like to boast about their achievements in destruction, and the only reason they have succeeded thus far is because we believers have not forcefully advanced the kingdom of God in these areas.

These enemy attacks can actually be turned around to be opportunities to show how great God is in *every* situation and circumstance! Be inspired today as you read what we have learned and experienced as a family. May confidence in God's Word rise up inside of you. May you have a childlike faith to believe God for something big to happen in your body, family, and work life. May you experience the great joy that comes from great victory!

CHAPTER 1

Pursue and Recover All

We have an enemy who enjoys dominating and diminishing our lives so that they become less than the abundant lives God has provided through Jesus Christ, our Lord and Savior. The Devil is a determined and fierce enemy who uses schemes and people to take away from us all we can enjoy from God. He doesn't want us to experience the joy of seeing our children mature into godly people with purpose and fulfillment, so he targets them for destruction. He makes attempts every day to break through the barriers of safety and protection surrounding our families. But the Devil cannot succeed with his plans if we are fulfilling our God-given destinies and achieving success through our leadership roles. Therefore he must put hindrances in our paths to stop us or at least slow us down.

We cannot ignore the existence of this enemy. Those who do ignore him become easy prey. We also must be mindful of the fact that our God, who is the Creator of all things, including the Devil, has given us *everything* we need to defeat him in *every* situation. First Samuel 30 gives us the account of how the Devil attacked David using the Amalekites and how David responded. This Scripture gives us great, propelling insight into the victory stories that follow.

David and his men had been fighting and defeating their fierce enemy, the Philistines. In fact, we are told they had been winning victory after victory. They had just returned to Ziklag, their home base, only to discover that the Amalekites had captured all of their wives and children. They had also taken all of their possessions and destroyed what was left by fire. The Amalekites were a longtime enemy that God had ordered King Saul to destroy earlier, but King Saul had not followed the instruction of the Lord. Now they had taken advantage of David's absence and organized an attack that would strip David and his soldiers of everything good in their lives. All their possessions and loved ones had been taken by the enemy! David and his men were filled with grief. The Scriptures describe the scene in this way: "They wept until they had no more power to weep" (v. 4).

It's important to remember that you can be fighting an enemy, winning battle after battle, and then suddenly a different, fierce enemy that was never fully annihilated can appear and actually do great damage. You can be fighting autism in your child and suddenly adultery will ravage your marriage, leaving you overwhelmed with grief. Never underestimate these enemies that thrive on destroying our very lives in any way they can.

The Bible also tells us that the men did exactly what a lot of us are tempted to do in times of great trial and heartache: they looked for someone to blame. Instead of dealing with the heart of the matter, the real enemy, they let their grief turn into rage. The men who fought alongside David and who believed in his godly leadership now hated him so much that they wanted to kill him. Now David was suffering from not only his own personal loss but also blame, guilt, and the threat of death.

Here's another great truth to remember: the Devil always, always, always piles on a lot of problems—big and small—from all directions to cause you to be depressed, feeling alone and truly isolated, so you will respond with a pathetic "what's the use" attitude. If he can get you to shrink back in confidence and draw back from prayer, then he has the victory. That is why God's Word basically tells us over and over again, "Don't fear. Don't get discouraged. Don't fret." A great Scripture to remember is Hebrews 10:35: "Do not cast away your confidence, which has great reward." In other words, keep standing right where you are in faith, believing God for something big to happen.

David's men had decided to get relief from their suffering by finding someone else to blame, not realizing that this is a false comfort and only a temporary solution. Don't fall for that tactic. You will wear yourself out emotionally and physically and bring further isolation. People are not your problem. Keep your attention on the real enemy. That enemy is unseen.

Let's look at what the Scripture tells us about David's response: "But, David strengthened himself in the Lord his God. So, David inquired of the Lord" (1 Sam. 30:6, 8). This tells us that when we are under great stress and suffer loss, our strength will come when we turn to someone greater than the circumstance and the people around us, and that someone is our great God. When David went into the presence of God and inquired of him, he didn't say, "Oh, Lord, my God, can you help me cope with this stress? Oh, great God in heaven and earth, will you help me get through this day?" No. This man of faith prayed a bold prayer to God that showed respect to just how great our God is, and he boldly said, "Shall I pursue this troop? Shall I overtake them?" God answered back, "Pursue, for you shall surely overtake them and recover all!" (v. 8).

Mighty men and women of God, when you are facing multifaceted problems like David, find your strength by going into the presence of God and inquiring of Him—not to recover *some,* but to recover *all*! Pursue the enemy that has stolen your mate, your children, your house, and your goods. Ask the Lord to help you and to bring you success. Ask the Lord for His power to recover everything! It's time to believe God for something big!

Have you lost your children to drug addiction? Has divorce ravaged your family? Have financial problems caused grief and loss? Then pray a bold prayer and ask God to help you pursue these powerful enemies and recover all. Pray a prayer worthy of the sacrifice that has been made for us when Jesus Christ suffered so greatly, dying on the cross for our sins and then rising again from the grave to give good gifts to men! Pray a prayer to achieve big victory in the mighty name of Jesus, and see for yourself that God will grant you great success!

When you have this kind of faith, an interesting thing will happen. Everything changes! People will change. All those men who were so angry with David and ready to kill him had a heart change to where they *once again* marched into battle with David to recover all their belongings! What happened? If you will trust that God will give you success in recovering all that has been captured by the enemy, then God will change the hearts of the people and give you help in pursuing the enemy. Faith like this attracts people to your way of thinking. You become a leader of men. The moment you decide to respond like David did (inquire of the Lord and pursue all), God will send you all the help you need to achieve success, even changing the hearts and attitudes of people who were once against you! Amazing!

This is why you should not lose your focus by concentrating on people's opinions of you at the time of crisis. It will weaken you, and you may discover that the opinions have changed. By the time you figure this out, you will be too tired to fight the real enemy, who has not changed at all in his constant driving hatred for you. Think about David and his six hundred men again. They finally started pursuing the enemy, but two hundred of them were too exhausted and couldn't go the full distance to destroy the enemy, so they stayed at Besor Ravine. The Hebrew meaning for the word *Besor* is "a place of cheerfulness and a place to be refreshed." They were to remain there and be repaired emotionally as well as physically.

If you insist on dealing with problems by blaming someone else, being mad, holding grudges, and being irritated, then much time will be required to get yourself built back up emotionally and physically. While everyone else is pursuing and recovering all, you'll be too weak and faint to go the distance. If you are going to regain your strength, you're going to have to take a rest from all those harmful emotions and start thinking about what is true and lovely (cheerful), letting yourself be refreshed.

So many times, when a loved one is in the hospital, the family should be pursing the enemy of disease, but instead they are engaged in battle with the doctor or a nurse who might have come in one time and was having a bad day. The family will exert all their strength on that person while letting the real enemy escape with their loved one. Don't let this happen to you. Keep your focus, and don't get sidetracked.

As we read on in 1 Samuel, God took this multifaceted

problem, this overwhelming loss, and turned it into a glorious victory. It just so happened, as they began their pursuit, that they met an Egyptian who not only exposed what the enemy, the Amalekites, had done, but also where they were. You will find that when you inquire of the Lord and eagerly desire His instruction on your problem, the Holy Spirit will reveal to you the exact enemy, his location, and his entire plan.

The Scriptures tell us that God provided this "messenger," who led them right into the enemy's camp, and there they were eating, drinking, partying, and enjoying all the plunder they had taken. It's interesting that the messenger then made David promise to not kill him once he revealed all this. Maybe that is where we get the saying, "Don't shoot the messenger," and that should probably be emphasized today—particularly every time a Christian hears a diagnosis from a doctor. The doctor is simply exposing where the enemy is and what he is doing. It's up to you to determine what you're going to do about it. Like David, it's up to you to fight with all your might. The Scriptures say that "David attacked them from twilight until the evening of the next day" (v. 17).

It's not enough to just identify the enemy. Be prepared to fight and totally destroy him. David kept fighting no matter how long it took. We know that he was fighting with a fierce determination when we read the outcome: "Nothing of theirs was lacking, either small or great, sons or daughters, spoil or anything which they had taken from them. He recovered all" (v. 19). In other words, he didn't let them hang on to one single thing they had taken! If disease is racing through your body, drive it out, and do not let it have one single organ, muscle, or cell! If addiction is plundering your family members, drive it out, and do not allow it to have one single member or to step foot in your house! If debt is destroying your reputation and livelihood, then put a stop to it, and don't quit until you don't owe anybody anything! You become the lender and not the borrower. David went from having absolutely nothing to being absolutely rich in just twenty-four hours! That financial turnaround happened because he decided to believe God for something big.

The Scriptures say that David *attacked* the enemy, and the Hebrew word used here is *nakah*. It means to *strike, beat, give wounds, and give stripes*. Isn't it interesting that this is what happened to Jesus when he suffered for us? They beat him, would strike him with their fists, gave him wounds, and laid stripes on his back. You and I are to take the victory that Jesus won by way of the cross and repeatedly strike, beat, and wound our enemy with the powerful name of Jesus! With the same tenacity that David had in physically fighting his enemy that day, we say to our enemy, "Get out! In the name of Jesus!" Every time you see the presence of your enemy, whether it be disease or godless behavior, you say, "In the name of Jesus, I drive you out of my body, my family, and my situation!"

In this way, you will be like David. David brought everything back! It gave him a great confidence in what the power of God could enable him to do. In Psalm 18, David describes the victory that God gave him over his enemies. "For by you I can run against a troop. By my God I can leap over a wall" (v. 29). He points out near the end of the Psalm, "I have pursued my enemies and overtaken them; neither did I turn back again till they were destroyed" (v. 37). David encouraged future generations all through his writings to have the same faith in God and discover how faithful He is to His Word. You will experience the great turnaround just like he did. Decide today to believe God for something big.

CHAPTER 2

Don't Let Disease Boast

My father had just started a new church in Ohio. He had been a denominational pastor for years and had started two churches that were still very well established and flourishing. But now he felt the call of God to start a church that was nondenominational and give the Holy Spirit complete freedom and leadership. We decided that we would not restrict the Holy Spirit and make Him follow traditions of men. Instead, we would follow *His* leadership. The adventure we experienced as a family and a church was phenomenal. We learned so much about the Holy Spirit and His ways. We experienced many miracles and were strengthened in our faith on every level.

About five years after we started, my father had told me one day that he was suffering from pain in his foot, especially his toe. Some time went by and the pain was getting more severe. He told me that he had gone to see a doctor and was being treated for gout. One morning I was talking to him on the phone, and he told me he was just in terrible misery with his foot and it was very red. I prayed with him on the phone, but

I was still troubled when we hung up. I began praying in my heavenly language about the situation. Soon my sister, Mary Ellen, who has been a medical flight nurse for years, called me. She told me that she had just talked with Dad at length about his foot and that I needed to take him to the emergency room right away. She also told me that she was convinced that he had a diabetic ulcer in his foot and not gout. Even though Dad had not been diagnosed as a diabetic, we had noticed that he had some signs indicating the presence of diabetes. She then warned me, "Lee, the first thing they are going to want to do is amputate. Don't let that happen. Let's decide right now for Dad's total recovery!" I was alarmed, but we agreed right then and there on the phone for the outcome.

I hurried as fast as I could to get Dad to the emergency room. I could tell his thinking and perception on everything, including my driving skills, were not rational. When the doctor pulled up my dad's pant leg and removed his sock, I gasped in horror because his leg was deep red up to the knee! I knew at that moment that Mary Ellen had revealed to me who the enemy was and what he was doing.

It was a long day of hearing that Dad was indeed diabetic and his sugar level had been extremely elevated for a long time, producing not just one ulcer but three! He was also very close to a heart attack due to blockage in his arteries. My dad was very sick, scared, and heavily medicated. His fate was in our hands. It was now up to us to put into practice everything we had learned from our parents.

From as early as I can remember, whenever we drove in the car, dad would tell us of miracles that happened in answer to prayer. He would tell us the stories more than once so that we would always remember how great God is. I learned at an early age from my parent's stories that God was able and willing to do great things because He loves us. One time, Dad was very discouraged and was ready to quit the Bible school he was attending in Georgetown, Kentucky. They just didn't have enough money to live on. He was offered an invitation to pastor a church in Rockford, Illinois, but it would mean that he would have to drop out of school.

Mom and Dad had not told anyone about their financial situation or the invitation. They prayed and agreed that if no money came in, then that was a sign from God that he was to accept the invitation to go to Rockford and pastor the church. Some time went by, and there wasn't enough money to buy milk for me, their first baby. So, Dad decided, with a heavy heart, to mail his acceptance letter to the church. As he leaned over to get the letter off the car seat to mail, the letter was gone and in its place was a plain envelope that had *Dave* written on it. Inside was a five-dollar bill! It was enough to buy milk, and more importantly it was exactly what Dad needed so that he would know that God wanted him to stay. Doors soon opened for Dad to have a good paying job at a grocery store as well as an invitation to pastor an established church in Kentucky.

There were many times that Dad would experience God's great hand of mercy on him. When Dad first began to preach, he pastored a church in Groveport, Ohio, and every Sunday night would drive hundreds of miles back to Kentucky. One night he was completely exhausted and fell asleep at the wheel. But God was watching over him and He woke Dad up, keeping him from an accident. On another occasion, Mom had been cleaning house while Dad was outside washing the car. Mom had the fireplace going and a space heater turned on as well. She was becoming very ill and sleepy. Dad just happened to come back into the house and realized that carbon monoxide fumes had filled the apartment. He quickly removed Mom from the house before she was completely overcome with the fumes. Once again, the Lord had prevented a tragedy.

Recalling these testimonies, in my heart I just knew that God would help my dad now in the hour of his greatest need, and it was up to me to get into the presence of God and find out His plan. So, when I came home, I went into our basement with my Bible in my hand, and I started praying to God in my heavenly language. I would open my Bible and let my eyes fall on whatever Scripture passage He wanted me to see until I heard his voice. Suddenly I heard His voice so distinctly, and He said, "What seems to be a disaster will turn out to be deliverance." I then knew that whatever I was going to face tomorrow would not compare to the Word of God He had spoken to my heart. I carried His Word with confidence as I walked into that hospital.

The Lord had also given me an understanding of my enemy, diabetes, when I read the Scriptures in Exodus 15:9. Just like the enemy the Israelites were facing that day at the Red Sea, I was facing an enemy who was boasting, "I will pursue, I will overtake, I will divide the spoil; my desire shall be satisfied on them. I will draw my sword. My hand shall destroy them." The disease, diabetes, boasts of pursuing people and draws its sword to destroy their limbs. But God has a way of dealing with these enemies. I was reading my New Living Translation that day, and I happened to turn to another Scripture passage in Isaiah 43:17: "I called forth the mighty army of Egypt with all its chariots and horses. I drew them beneath the waves and they drowned, their lives snuffed out like a smoldering candlewick." These words really got my attention and I understood what was happening. God showed me that diabetes had been there lurking and pursuing Dad for quite some time, and it was God who exposed this enemy so it could be stopped and destroyed! How did God annihilate the enemy of the Israelites that day? It was with His breath. He snuffed them out like a candlewick. The breath of God blew on those waters and created a path of escape for the people of God. The breath of God blew, and the same waters drowned their enemies. The power is in the breath of God. The breath of God, His Word, was giving me a path of deliverance for Dad. The breath of God, his Word, will also destroy diabetes, and it will not be able to boast concerning my dad.

Sure enough, all we heard for days was that the leg needed to be amputated, and the longer we waited we would be shortening Dad's life. Meanwhile, both of my sisters, Mary Ellen and Laura Mae, were searching for information concerning a new treatment for diabetic ulcers being used at a different hospital. The treatment involved using pressurized oxygen for wound healing. Laura Mae was in medical school at the time, and God brought her in contact with a young resident who had a thorough knowledge of the treatment. His senior doctor was on vacation, but he contacted him for us and then spent many hours researching for us everything we needed to know in order to see if Dad was a candidate. We were certain as a family that this was the path to choose, but trying to get the current hospital to release him to the other hospital was going to be a challenge.

Every day, while they were gathering information, my stepmother, Rita, and I would speak to Dad's foot. We continually spoke to the infection and ulcers to leave in the name of Jesus. The stench of death was in the room, and it would take every ounce of faith we had in God to not weaken into fear. We had to constantly encourage one another in God's Word and remind ourselves that God is faithful if we will continue to believe, no matter what it looks like. The Devil even tried to get Rita off by herself to where she would succumb to pressure. She was constantly getting a bad report on Dad's status in order to make a panic decision and agree to the amputation. But Rita held on to her faith and did not cave in. Rita had amazing faith day after day!

It's important to tell you that from the beginning there were many times to get angry with a nurse or even a doctor over the quality and manner that care was being delivered. But this is what God showed us from the beginning: Do not lose focus on who the real enemy is. We never once had an argument with anyone and conducted ourselves worthy of the gospel, even though we were facing one of the biggest challenges of our lives. We also listened intently and gave our respect to everyone. After all, the medical team is simply reporting what they have discovered will happen if you don't do anything different than anybody else. The moment you do something different than anyone else, whether good or bad, statistics and probabilities change. We believed, like David, that we could pursue this enemy and recover all. But we did not share with everyone what we believed or what we were doing as a family. We were in an environment where it would have been construed as denial or being overzealous.

During all this time, Dad was heavily medicated and really didn't know what was going on. One night we received a hysterical call from Dad. He had evidently awakened suddenly to overhear the doctors discussing that they were going to amputate his leg. We all rushed in to comfort Dad and make

13

sure that the hospital knew that we were not approving any surgery. In the early morning hours, the surgeon came in with his team. They were dressed in their scrubs and were determined to take Dad in for surgery to amputate his leg. We were determined as a family to get Dad admitted to the other hospital for his first hyperbaric oxygen treatment. Laura Mae had spoken to the doctors working in that unit of the other hospital, and they had agreed that if we could get him there by four o'clock that afternoon, they would do an assessment. It was possible that treatment could begin immediately.

We were all gathered in the room with the surgeon and his team. It was a facing off of belief systems, and you could feel the tension. The surgeon started talking to us in a firm tone, warning us of being in denial and that Dad's life was now at risk if we waited one minute longer. We all started praying in the Spirit under our breath as my sister, Laura Mae, spoke to the surgeon.

She was eloquent as she explained that my father's quality of life was dependent upon his standing and walking because of the calling on his life. I'll never forget how you could *feel* the disarming of the enemy as he was laying down his weapons. She convincingly stated all the published positive results of the new hyperbaric (pressurized) oxygen treatment being conducted at the other hospital for people with similar conditions. She explained that they had agreed to do an assessment of Dad this very afternoon and even give him his first hyperbaric treatment if we could transfer him there by four o'clock. Finally, she said, "If this was your dad, wouldn't you want to do everything within your power to help him so that there would be no regrets?" At that, the surgeon said, "Yes, I would. I'll release him now." It was a great victory!

But now we had only a short time to get Dad over to the other hospital, and we had no time to wait for an ambulance to come. Laura Mae said, "Well, I can drive him." The surgeon was not in favor of that, but Dad suddenly rose up in his bed (from somewhat of a stupor) and shouted, "Patient's rights!" With that, Laura Mae and I drove him over to the hospital where he was quickly assessed and had his first treatment!

That night we also discovered that Dad now had four ulcers in his foot! A vascular surgeon had to cut out all the ulcers and left just a skeleton of a foot. But God's Word was able to not only remove all the dead tissue and infection but also restore healthy flesh. Today my father is written up in the books of the hyperbaric oxygen unit of that hospital as a *walking miracle*. Diabetes was not able to boast that it took a leg or even a toe! His foot is completely intact and functional.

The Word that God had given me at the beginning of that trial came true in so many ways. "What seems to be a disaster will turn out to be deliverance." The capillaries around dad's heart received so much oxygen from the hyperbaric treatments that they formed a natural bypass correcting the problem of blocked arteries. So, in fact, God saved his life by showing us how to treat his foot.

We learned so much through that ordeal. Truths were embedded in us so that we were able to walk with a greater strength. We were able to help our church family have a better understanding of how to stand on God's Word and believe God for something big.

Don't let diseases boast. Use the Word of God and the name of Jesus to destroy their power.

CHAPTER 3

There's Always a Way with Jesus

On Sunday and Wednesday nights, our little church would gather around a table and have a Bible lesson followed by prayer. Dad and I would have everyone open their Bibles as we read a passage of Scripture. We would then spend some time applying it to our everyday lives and invited prayer requests. So many miracles took place at that table with just a handful of people.

One night we received a desperate phone call from a family just as we were about to pray. Their little eight-year-old daughter had been diagnosed with a flesh-eating disease, and she was scheduled to have her leg amputated the next morning. As a family, we knew exactly how to talk to this disease, and now we had a group of people who were of the same mind and faith as us! We all began to pray with fervent prayer commanding this flesh-eating disease to leave her immediately, and we called in new bacteria-free flesh. We also prayed that the plans of the doctors would change.

The next day the family called my dad, the pastor, and

said that the doctors came in and decided to wait another day. As the week went by, each day the surgery was put off until another day. Our prayer was continually working against the enemy. One morning the little girl told her family, "Jesus came into my room last night." Soon the diagnosis was, "Nothing to worry about. It was just a cat scratch." She went home whole, and today she is a beautiful young Christian lady with a strong, healthy, intact body and a strong faith in God!

Years later, some relatives in that same family had another alarming incident. Their teenage daughter did not return home from high school. Hours had gone by and the father, a strong Christian, had asked that our church pray with him as he pursued to recover his daughter. After many phone calls to friends and school officials, they discovered that their daughter and a girlfriend had climbed into a truck with a stranger in the school parking lot. Her father was given a vague description of the truck by someone who just happened to be passing by as it happened. Our church called our prayer warriors and had them commanding the Devil to release the girls in the name of Jesus! Meanwhile, her father started walking up and down the streets of the neighborhood, relying on the Lord to direct him to the exact location of his daughter. As he walked, he was asking everyone he saw if they had seen the truck. One man said, "I think that is the truck across the street, but be careful because there are a bunch of tough guys who live there."

He quickly had his wife call 911 and alert the police, but this father, full of the power of God, walked boldly up to the front door of this house of thugs! As he did, fear struck the men, and they quickly released the girls out the back door. The girls came right up to the father, but they were acting very strangely. The police suddenly arrived and were amazed at the boldness of the father. Later he learned that the two innocent girls, who had never given their parents any reason for alarm, had been lured into the truck by very evil men and had been given powerful drugs. Everyone realized that if the father had not pursued this enemy, believing that God would help him have success, he would probably never have seen his innocent daughter again.

I often wonder how many of these wonderful stories would have had a completely different ending if we had not met our challenge with Dad the way we did. If we had just accepted the outcome of him losing his foot or leg to amputation, we would have been conducting our Bible lessons and prayer sessions a lot differently. We would have probably encouraged the people in our church to just accept whatever happens to them. Our prayers with them would consist of asking God to sustain them and help them through this tragedy of losing the young girl's leg. We would have asked the Lord to give them comfort over the loss of their daughter's innocence and/or life and help them through their grief. I am so grateful that God gave us His grace to pray boldly like David and dare to believe Him for something big. It changed our lives and the lives of those in our circle of influence.

Remember this, as you feel faith rise in your heart: the decision of faith you make today will affect not only you but all of your family and all those you come in contact with from this day forward. You will be just as influential as David was with the 600 men and their families. What a difference one man's faith can make!

CHAPTER 4

The Power of the Cross

Everybody has the potential to be a great man or woman of faith. God has given us everything we need in order to have godly character and win victories in any arena. It really is simply a matter of knowing what He has provided for us and using those provisions. When we do something other than that, we start losing ground and giving way to doing things without God's approval. Anything that God doesn't approve of is going to result in harm and lots of hurt. It would be wonderful if every believer would just follow God's Word and pray about everything.

The greatest times of grief in my life were caused because I didn't pray and seek God's counsel, or if I did, I had found a reason to reject it. What followed was a series of bad decisions that were influenced by ungodly sources. Sadly, that's a scenario played out too many times in the lives of many Christians who love the Lord. When we come to a dry, desert place in our lives, we don't seek the Lord for our next plan of action. We start getting irritable, complaining about everybody and everything around us. Pretty soon we are making bad decisions left and right and letting words come out of our mouths that invite trouble. Our behavior is almost exactly like the Israelites when they came to Marah and the water was bitter. It was so bitter, they couldn't drink it or use it for their livestock.

They didn't remind themselves of the great victory that God had given them when he brought them out of Egypt. They didn't remember how God drowned Pharaoh and his army in the Red Sea. God had become very small in their eyes—so small that He couldn't take care of a little problem like water tasting bitter. So, they grumbled and complained and let their mouths slander God and His goodness to them. Their speech was harsh and full of regret, "We should have done this and we should have done that!" Godless chatter is all it was. When Moses approached God and asked Him what they were to do, the Scriptures say that God simply "showed him a tree." When Moses threw that tree in the water it made bitter water sweet. Everyone was able to drink the water and be satisfied. God then made a bold proclamation, a law for them and every generation to follow. It was basically this: Listen to me and do what I say. This is the Scripture in Exodus 15, where God declares, "I am the God that healeth thee."

There will be times in our journey in this life when the waters may be bitter. But God has given us the same insight that He gave Moses that day: our answer is that tree on Calvary where Jesus suffered and died in our place. Apply that tree to your situation and expect it to change from bitter to sweet. What happened on that tree that day has enough power to overcome every sin, every sickness, and every situation. We sing songs about the cross, about the blood, and about the power made available to us that day to overcome the enemy of our souls. We do this to remind ourselves that Jesus was crucified on that tree for us, and every drop of blood shed that day was enough for every one of our needs. Remember the cross. Remember the tree.

I love to read that passage of Scripture in Exodus 15 because the very last verse states, "Then they came to Elim, where there were twelve wells of water and seventy palm trees." They were only seven miles away from a place where there was plenty of water and lots of shade. Why didn't God say to Moses, "Just keep going, dummy! You'll come to it!"

God wanted them to see that if He *said* there was power in the tree to turn bitter water sweet, then there *was indeed* power in the tree to turn bitter water sweet! God wants you and me to know that He decided Jesus would be crucified on the tree, and He decided that it was there that sin would be defeated. It was God who decided that Jesus' name would be glorified so that at that name every knee must bow. If God says *there is* power in that tree, then it *does indeed* have power! Use that power to change your situation! Just believe it and do it. Here's the best part: right around the corner, a short distance away, is all the water you need, and more. Our great God, who not only "supplies all our needs" (Phil. 4:19), but is also "able to do exceedingly abundantly above all that we ask or think, according to the power that works in us" (Eph. 3:20), will provide shade trees as well.

Don't live your life without ever experiencing the joy of listening to God and doing what He says. It's a wonderful feeling to please God by letting Him counsel you and then see everything turn out just right! What a sad existence to just go from crisis to crisis and never once exercise your faith in God's Word and expect an answer to prayer. You'll be as miserable as the Israelites were. Just one month later, after leaving that beautiful place of wells and shade trees, they came to another *desert place* and started that whole routine over again of complaining instead of praying. It's like that saying, "Some people have to learn the hard way."

This time the Israelites were craving food. They were craving bread and meat and needed lots of it. Instead of building on what they had already learned and experienced with God—that they could believe Him for something big—they implemented the *tried that and failed miserably* plan of griping, complaining, and criticizing Moses and the other leadership. Once again, Moses went into the presence of God and asked Him what to do. God gave him a simple solution to this big problem that everyone was so worked up about. This story, as told in Exodus 16, is so exciting to read because it shows us the very personality of God. God loves to take a situation that the Devil has portrayed as impossibly big and solve it with a very small simple solution. He does this to show us what a deceiver the Devil is.

The people were all upset. They were mad at Moses and thought they were going to die in the wilderness. This problem had become so huge that everyone was upset and angry with everyone else. Even Moses and Aaron had had enough of the people constantly complaining about their leadership. So, when this *huge* problem was brought to God's attention, He didn't have to ponder it over and see what He could come up with. God just said, in essence, "Okay, tonight you will have meat, and in the morning you will have bread." Problem solved. I can just imagine how Moses must have looked when God gave this very simple answer to him. It shocked him so much that Moses actually started trying to figure out how God was going to do it.

In Numbers 11:21, the Scriptures gives us a little behind-the-scenes look with Moses and God. Moses says, "The people whom I am among are six hundred thousand men on foot and yet you have said, 'I will give them meat that they may eat for a whole month!' Shall flocks and herds be slaughtered for them? Or shall all the fish of the sea be gathered together for them, to provide enough for them?" The Lord answered Moses, "Has the Lord's arm been shortened?" It's almost like God is saying, "Hey, Moses, did I lose my power? Did something happen that now I can't do whatever I have decided to do? I created all the fish in the sea and the birds in the air, and now you don't think I have the power to take what I created and fulfill a need?"

There have certainly been times in my life when I received a well-deserved *heart check* from the Lord just to show me how small my thinking had become. This conversation is very similar to the one Jesus had with Philip when there were five thousand men and their families to feed. In John 6:5, the Scriptures tell us that Jesus already knew what He was going to do when He saw the great crowd, but He asked Philip a question to see where his faith was. Philip responded like Moses: "Two hundred *denarii* (which was eight months wages at that time) worth of bread is not sufficient for them, that every one of them may have a little" (John 6:7). These Scriptures let us know that it is really easy to respond to crises like Moses and Philip. Many years separated these two great men of God, and many years separate us from them. However, despite all the knowledge and experience of God's way that have been accumulated, we can still be as easily influenced by small thinking as these mighty men all those centuries ago.

In Psalms 78, a song was written that really sums up what happened to the people of God when they came to that desert place. In Psalm 78:11, the Scripture tells us that they "forgot His works and His wonders that He had shown them ... He split the rocks in the wilderness, and gave them drink in abundance like the depths" (v. 15).

> "He also brought streams out of the rock and caused water to run down like rivers: (v. 16).

> "Yet, they spoke against God: they said, 'Can God prepare a table in the wilderness?'"(v. 19).

> "'Behold, he struck the rock, so that water gushed out, and the streams overflowed. Can he give bread also? Can he provide meat for his people?'" (v. 20).

Don't let that kind of thinking rob you of enjoying the abundant life God wants all of us to have. Don't say, "Sure, He forgave me of all my sins and saved me but, can He heal my body?" or, "Sure, He healed my body, but can He give me money as well? Can God really supply *all* my needs?" The answer is "Yes!"

This Psalm also lets us know how insulting this way of thinking is to God. God was very angry with them because "they did not believe in God, and did not trust in His salvation" (v. 22). Psalm 78 continues on, telling us that God simply "commanded the clouds above, and opened the doors of heaven" (v. 23). He rained down bread and meat! It also tells us that it wasn't just a little bit. He sent them *all* the food they needed! At God's command, the quail was made to come down into their camp, all around their tent, and they had more than enough! Not only can God spread a table of abundant supply in the desert, but He also has the power to make it all come right to your door!

All these Scriptures tell us that God has very simple solutions to big problems. What we think is overwhelming and impossible, God has the power to remove and change, even instantly. The answer to every problem we face is to go into God's presence and get His instructions. Notice that these solutions relied on God's power, not on the power of Moses, Philip, or any human being. There are problems that simply must have God solutions, and all the man power in the world is not going to change a thing!

When was the last time you had the ability to open the heavens and rain down groceries for your family? Have you ever hit a rock and your entire state flooded with water? But those are the kind of things that God does effortlessly, and all He asks us to do is believe that He can and will do it! We all think about the great event when God parted the Red Sea, but God parted the Jordan for Joshua and parted it again for Elisha! My dad has always said to us, "God parts rivers and seas like I do my hair!" Nothing is too hard for him! If you believe God for something big to happen, He'll do it and enjoy it … but you have to believe it.

CHAPTER 5

God is Greater Than You Think He Is

Remember the man whose little boy was having seizures and he brought him to the disciples? This story is packed with great insight as to how the Devil works and how he draws strength. The complete story can be understood as you read the three passages in Matthew 17, Mark 9, and Luke 9.

Before Jesus arrived on the scene, there was a terrible ruckus. The teachers of the law were arguing with the disciples, the father was angry with the disciples for not being able to help his son, and there was a large crowd all around them. Meanwhile, his little boy was suffering and oppressed. Now, if you want to have an atmosphere where the Devil can really do a performance, this is it. He loves fussing and arguing. He loves it when people are feeling angry and hurt. He also loves an audience! They might as well have built a stage. The Devil then was able to put on a first-class performance, trying to deceive this audience into thinking that he was *the* superior being with supernatural undefeatable power!

When Jesus walked up to them, He first dealt with the arguing. Jesus wanted to know what it was that had gathered such a large crowd. The father answered (Matt. 17:15, 16), "My son is epileptic and suffers severely … I brought him to your disciples, but they could not *cure* him." In Mark 9:17 the father answered, "My son who has a *mute spirit* …" In Luke 9:39 the father answers, "A *spirit seizes* him … I spoke to your disciples, that they could *cast it out*, but they could not." Perhaps this big important discussion, which led to the community argument, was, "Is it a demon or is it not a demon? Is the child demon possessed or just oppressed?" The exact ecumenical answers may never result in anything other than division and feeding the Devil's ego. He loves to be the center of attention.

Both Mark and Luke point out something else as well. The father goes on and on to Jesus telling him all about the mighty exploits of this sickness/demon. He tells Jesus that it seizes him, and he suddenly screams. It throws him into convulsions so that he foams at the mouth. He gnashes his teeth and becomes rigid. He falls into fire and water. It scarcely ever leaves him and is destroying him. Now, at first glance, it looks like he's just explaining that there's a real problem here, in the same way that we would tell our symptoms to a doctor. But keep in mind the father is standing in the presence of Jesus Christ, the one sent from God to be our Messiah—the one sent from God Himself to perform mighty and powerful miracles on our behalf. That is why he brought his son to Jesus in the first place. So, he is standing in the presence of Jesus, the answer to his prayer, but because he has been talking up the problem and giving accolades to the workmanship of the Devil, his faith diminishes. He then makes a weak and pathetic statement to Jesus, "But, if you can do anything, have compassion on us and help us" (Mark 9:22).

Jesus immediately responds, "If I can?" I can just imagine the expression on the face of Jesus at that moment. Frankly, I have done the very same dumb thing in my own Christian life. I have thought about and meditated on a problem so much, seeing it from all angles, that by the time I got into the presence of the Lord, I felt totally defeated. My prayer of faith consisted of, "Well, can you just remove this headache?" I forgot who I was talking to. It is so easy to forget that I am in the presence of Jesus, "[who] saw Satan fall like lightning and that [I] should rejoice that my name is written in Heaven! He has given [me] authority to trample on serpents and scorpions and over all the power of the enemy and nothing shall by any means harm [me]!" (Luke10:18, 19).

Jesus declared to that father, and it's still true for us today, "Nothing is impossible for him who believes!" As usual, this seemingly big problem was solved instantly by the power of God. In Luke 9:42 the Scripture says, "Jesus rebuked the unclean spirit, healed the child, and gave him back to his father." If it's an evil spirit that needs to be driven out, or if it's a sickness that needs to be healed, God has got you covered! He can get everything right back to the way it needs to be. That passage goes on to say, "They were all amazed at the majesty of God."

Remember, the Scriptures tell us that the Devil's ambition from the very beginning was to be as big as God. He declared, "I will make myself like the Most High" (Isa. 14:13 NIV). That is exactly what he tries to deceive us into believing. He tries to make it appear that his abilities and weaponry are as big as

God's. The truth is that it's all smoke and mirrors, all deception, and there will be a day, as stated in verse 16, when we will see him for what he is and say, "Is this the one who made the earth tremble, who shook kingdoms, who made the world as a wilderness and destroyed its cities?"

When you first come face-to-face with a sickness, disease, demon spirit, or even a person being used as a device of Satan, there is a strong urge to just cave in. Countless Christians have laid down the powerful weaponry God has given them—just start cowering down and concede to the enemy's demands. The Scriptures tell us story after story about when it has happened and how it brought failure every time. Kings would empty out their personal treasury—as well as God's treasury—to appease their attackers. It never accomplished a thing except to prolong the misery.

I have personally prayed with people and felt the power of God go into their loved one. The afflicted person and their family knew they were healed. But every day after that they would choose to believe something other than what God had said and done. They would call me and ask me about some article they read or a talk with a friend. Pretty soon a symptom or two would come, followed by a doctor's report. Next thing you know, the diagnosis is a *fact*, and God's Word spoken into them is totally discounted. Here's the key to receiving and holding on to your miracle: The Word God speaks to your situation must be counted as stronger and more authoritative, and it must be rehearsed in your heart and mind more than the diagnosis or what others say.

One day I was talking on the phone with a dear friend who had been sick for quite a long time. She went on and on for nearly an hour telling me what the doctors had said and what she had read about the sickness. Finally, I asked her what God had said to her and what Scripture was she standing on. There was almost silence as she stammered around for an answer. She did not have a single word from God or a specific Scripture. No wonder this very small pathetic sickness was lingering in her body and creating havoc! One day it will surprise us how we let such little things deceive us all because we "darkened God's counsel" and treated His wisdom like it was meaningless.

Oh, to be like young David—who believed God was greater than any lion or bear! Oh, to have the faith of that young man that when he saw that big giant, Goliath, he charged at him, armed with simply the name of the Lord! Once again, this big-mouth giant talked and talked for forty days and forty nights about how big and strong he was. Can you believe that these mighty men of God listened to him run off at the mouth that long—making fun of them and God every day? Yet we can be guilty of the same thing and just give all our attention to something that cannot compare to God and His power.

After forty days and forty nights of all this *big* talk, God answered him with a *little* boy, a *little* stone, and the *least of all weaponry* at that time ... a slingshot! It is so like God. He always takes the boasts of the enemy and just reduces them to where they're just a joke. Goliath found out that God is much greater than you may think He is!

CHAPTER 6

Go Ahead, God, and Just Be Who You Are

The biggest turnaround for our family came when we started listening to preaching that stimulated our faith to believe in God's Word as absolute truth in every situation for us today. Even though we read the Scriptures before then, we read it more as a history book telling us what had happened to others. When we started hearing how to take Scripture and believe it will come true for the situation that we were in, miracles started happening in every area of our lives.

My mom and dad have always instilled in us a respect for the men and women who preach God's Word. I'm so grateful for that because it has produced good soil in our hearts to receive from God's preachers. We were watching a well-known preacher on TV at our home one day with some friends. One friend was a bit of a mystery to us because his mom was a Christian and he had attended church most of his life, yet he was not really a spiritual person in many ways. While we were watching the show—which was so powerful that it had every one's attention—he was making comments about the preacher's hair or his shoes. Others looked at him as if to say, "Who cares?" At that moment we realized that he had never been taught to respect God's preachers.

Actually, it was very sad. He didn't know what it was like to have a very heavy heart and then go to a church service or turn on a television program where the man of God speaks a Word that goes right to the heart of the matter—a word so strong and authoritative that it is no longer a man speaking, but it is the Lord talking straight to your heart using that man's vocal chords.

When I was young and foolish, I would say, "Well, I really don't care for this preacher or that one. They don't do much for me." Then one day, I walked in the door of my home. I was very depressed over what had happened at work. I turned on the TV just in time to hear one of those preachers *that didn't do much for me* call out my name. It got my attention, and every word that came out of his mouth was as if God had been reading my mind! When he finished speaking, he had read my mail. I knew that God can and will use anybody at anytime to speak a Word to me when He wants to. He didn't need my opinion on who it should or should not be.

Once my grandma was in the hospital, and she had one of the most well-known heart specialists replacing her heart valve. On a Sunday morning, this very well-known, highly credentialed cardiologist walked into her room announcing that he wanted to talk to her about her heart. She immediately told him in a nice way, "We must be quiet now, the man of God is speaking." The cardiologist sat down beside her bed and gave the man of God his attention. When his colleague came in, he also had a seat and they all watched and listened together to the man of God. These men learned what all the children in our family had learned at an early age. There's not going to be any talking and carrying on while the man of God is speaking

My parents had prayed for a singer and a preacher. I was their firstborn, and it was apparent from the beginning that I had both those gifts. In fact, all three of their daughters sing and have the gift of preaching as well. I often sang in church, traveled with my dad to revival meetings, and even began writing songs at the age of twelve. When I graduated from high school, Mary Ellen and I started working at a steakhouse restaurant. My mom soon noticed that I was picking up a lot of ways of the world. I wasn't really doing anything wrong, but I was being influenced. She saw that even though I didn't cuss, I was talking with roughness. I was losing my temper more and being disagreeable most of the time. My mom became bothered in her spirit about me because she knew that I had a great calling on my life, and the Devil was starting to implement a plan to get me off the right path.

At the same time, my grandpa was in the hospital and was very sick with colon cancer. Mom went to visit him one day with a heavy burden concerning me. She started pouring out her heart to Grandpa about me. When she finished, Grandpa simply said, "Well, she needs to be in Bible college." Mom exclaimed, "Oh, Dad, I can't even talk to Linda Lee." Grandpa said, "Let's pray … you and me … and God will put her in the school." They prayed that bold prayer of faith right there in the hospital, even though Grandpa was so sick at the time.

Mom came home and found that I was not working that day. She said, "You need to go see your grandpa in the hospital." I reluctantly agreed to go back to the hospital with her to see

Grandpa. As we were driving, she took a route that went right past the Bible college. As we were approaching the school, she said, "Why don't we just go in and check it out. Let's just see what they offer." I protested that I was not interested in Bible school, but she finally convinced me to go in and check it out. It just so happened that the president was in his office, and he met with us personally. I knew that I was in the presence of a great man of God as he talked with my mother. I was amazed as I listened to him.

As he listened to my mom tell him about me singing, he said, "Well, we need to get you in the college choir. The choir director is here now, so let's have you do an audition with him!" Immediately, I was sent to the director for an audition. He was a very nice gentleman with a really pleasant way about him. He said, "Well, just sing something you know … how about 'Amazing Grace'?" I was thrilled and quickly agreed. I got about ten words out and could not remember another word of the song! I was totally embarrassed and shocked as was he, since everybody who has ever sung in church has probably sung that song at least a thousand times. It suddenly hit me like a brick, "What has happened to me that I don't even know the words to 'Amazing Grace'?" At that moment, *I knew* that I needed to be in Bible school! I was enrolled that day and had my first class that night. I also had the best time being a member of the college choir. That godly choir director gave me many opportunities to share my songwriting gift as well as my voice whenever we traveled. He was a very unique teacher and just what I needed.

Once again, God took a very big problem and solved it effortlessly by his awesome power! I'm so grateful that my mom and grandpa decided to believe God for something big. It changed my life!

I can tell you with confidence that if you have a son or daughter that is starting to stray, God can put him or her back on the right path. Just pray a bold prayer of faith and let God do the rest. Just as he did with me, He knows exactly what needs to happen in order to get him or her to want to be on that right path.

It was there at that little Bible college that I actually started reading my Bible. I started a habit of getting up early in the morning and reading the Scriptures. It changed my life so much that I have now done this for thirty-three years. My time in the morning with God's Word and letting the Holy Spirit talk to me as I read is the most precious intimate time I have with Him.

By the way, my grandpa was healed of that colon cancer. The doctors had said that it was a very aggressive cancer in a difficult place, and they were concerned that he would not be able to come through surgery. They intended to just relieve the obstruction. A preacher came into my grandpa's room, opened his Bible to Psalm 41, and prayed a powerful prayer full of God's promise in that Scripture. My grandpa had always been kind to the poor. He owned a grocery store and had a *regard for the weak*. The preacher quoted God's promise that "He would restore him from his bed of illness." After that prayer, the doctors decided to perform the surgery. The doctor told my grandpa that he just decided to get aggressive and cut out all the cancer. My grandpa recovered quickly and went home cancer free. He lived ten more years with no further treatment, and cancer did not claim him. When he went home to be with the Lord, he had lived a very satisfying life and had successfully passed on his strong faith in God to all of us in the next generations.

CHAPTER 7

God at Work

In my late twenties, I began working for a grocery store and was hired in as a sign maker. My job was to put tags with prices on the product and make signs for displays. I became very good at it and soon realized that not only was I a very good writer, but I was also fast. It became a secure position for me in the store. However, I had a desire to be a department manager and felt like I could do that job equally well. It just so happened that the home center department had become vacant, so I asked the manager if he would consider me for the department manager position. He shot down the idea immediately. He saw me as a sign maker, not a manager.

Well, I was reading the Scriptures as I did every morning before I started my workday, and I read in Deuteronomy 28 that God promised that if the people would listen to Him and obey His commands that *He* would make them the head and not the tail, above only and not beneath. I thought to myself, "I do that. I listen to the Lord speak to me every day and I read his Word every day and put it into practice ... so, that promise is for me." As I meditated on that Scripture, I'll never forget, I had just made a sign for potato chips and stepped across the aisle to hang it up. As I did, I decided in my heart and whispered to the Lord, "I am asking *you* to make me a department manager so that I am the head and not the tail."

Weeks went by and nothing seemed to be happening. All the while, I kept speaking that Scripture over and over to myself, "I am the head and not the tail," and I even wrote a song telling how it was going to come to pass. Then one day, just like the song, the supervisor came into the store and told me he had decided to make me the manager of the home center department! I was so thrilled, and I knew that it was God making His Word come true on my behalf!

While working at the grocery store, I experienced some wonderful miracles and answers to prayers. As I read the Word of God each day, God would show me a way to put into practice what I was reading. I read that I could "Say to the mountain, 'Be removed and be cast into the sea,' and it will be done" (Matt. 21:21). I was meditating on the fact that my words can bless and my words can curse. So I started paying attention to what I was saying.

The company had decided to upgrade our little store to be just like the others in the grocery store chain. All other stores had a lottery machine at the front of the store, near the office. They brought in a lottery machine. I began to notice that all my friends were putting their money into this machine when they would come up front to the office. Day after day they were just throwing their money away. It was money they had worked so hard to earn. Day after day, it really bothered me to see this happen. So, every day when I went to the office, I would just lean over toward the machine and place my hand on it while saying under my breath, "I curse you in the name of Jesus." Soon I noticed that the lottery machine was not working properly, and they would call in someone to repair it. After they repaired it, I placed my hand on it again and cursed it. It started having issues all the time and was in constant need of repair. Most of the time, there was an *Out of Order* sign on the front of the machine. I never let up and no one knew what I was doing. Finally, they took the machine out and we became the only store to not have a lottery machine!

God's Word works in any environment. While I worked for that grocery store chain, I saw many exciting things happen because I was learning to believe God for something big. I saw healings of all kinds. I saw promotions. I saw bad managers removed and good ones come in. I saw injustices revealed and good people vindicated.

I had a manager once who wanted to fire me. He had become angry with me when I challenged an injustice done to the cashiers. One of my friends in the office told me what he was doing to set a trap for me in order to fire me. I simply prayed and asked for God's protection. The manager had been with the company eight years and had a pretty good reputation with them, but one morning he overslept and came in late for work. That same morning all his supervisors happened to come in for an unexpected visit and they fired him on the spot! It shocked everyone. I knew that it was because of God's Word. What you plan for others will boomerang and happen to you.

Before I left to go into full-time ministry with my dad, I was promoted to front manager in one of their nicest stores. I was in charge of all the operations and departments when the store manager and assistant managers were not there. This particular night, I was closing the store and had a great group of workers.

One of our best workers was not feeling well at all and was going to have to go home. I just felt led to ask if he would let me pray for him. He agreed and told me he had a terrible headache. I just simply put my hand on his forehead and commanded the headache to leave him in the name of Jesus. All of a sudden I just blurted out, "And he will never have a headache again!" It kind of shocked me that I said that. When he looked up at me, he was very relieved and happy. He also proceeded to tell me that he has always suffered from migraine headaches, and many of his family members do as well!

I thought, "Oh, great! This was a big problem, not just a little headache!" But it was still just a little problem to God. Just because it had a name and a reputation did not make it bigger than God.

He finished his shift headache free. I saw him years later at a recording studio and asked if he had ever suffered again with headaches and he said, "No." I was thrilled to hear that he was considering a call into the ministry. You just never know who God wants you to influence and encourage in their faith.

CHAPTER 8

My Deer Story

It was a beautiful Sunday afternoon and several of us were sitting in the front yard of our country church. We noticed a family of deer in the field across from us, and we enjoyed watching them run and play. However, our "ahhs" quickly turned to "oohs" as we realized they were now running toward the highway. All the deer ran safely across the road except the last one.

We watched in horror as what seemed to be a small deer was hit by a truck and thrown into the air—it hit the ground with a thud. As three of us ran swiftly to the scene, the deer lifted his head one last time and took his last breath. The man and his son who were in the truck that hit him were unharmed and joined us at the scene. It was evident to all that the deer had died, but compassion just overwhelmed my fellow church member and me. I'm not sure who even started, but we both began commanding life to come into this deer! Even though there was blood from his nose and mouth, we kept praying and shouting, "Live!"

It seemed to be an eternity and there was absolutely no movement, but we had started something we were going to finish! Faith surged through us both as we stretched our hands out over that lifeless body and spoke the powerful promises of God. I will never forget that awesome moment when out of nowhere that deer just leaped to his feet! You have never seen such shocked looks on faces ... even the deer!

What was even more exciting is that this wild deer just stood there letting us pet and love on him while we praised God! Finally we had to push him off into the field saying, "Go! Run in Jesus' name!" It was as if he wanted to just stay there with us. As he ran into the field to join his family, he stopped briefly and looked back at us! It was a beautiful miracle!

I suddenly became aware of the man and his son who had been standing there the whole time. He looked at me and said simply, "That deer was dead." I said, "Yes, but now he's alive!" He began to tell me of a grave situation in his life that he had been praying about and said, "I don't understand why God answered your prayer and has not answered mine." I then knew why God had put us there that day and had moved us to pray and believe like we did. God wanted us to give this precious man valuable instruction so his prayer could be answered.

I said, "Did you see how we kept praying for that deer even though it looked like nothing was happening? We kept speaking the promises of God. We rebuked death and commanded life to come in the name of Jesus. We refused to give up, no matter how much time went by. If you will pray and if you refuse to give up, you will see things turn around!"

I will never forget my deer story, and God often reminds me to pray with the same fervency as I did that day—being

Linda Lee White

determined to get results. If you have a loved one overcome by alcohol, drugs, pornography, or sickness, I want to encourage you with this story. It may look like it's over and there's no life there anymore, but things can change completely. God is most interested in saving and salvaging the lives of men and women from death and destruction—not a deer. He cares about you and the things that concern you so very much. Pray and do not give up! Believe God for something big because He is willing and able. Today let faith swell up in your heart and believe God for something big!

Afterword

When my precious daughter, Linda Lee, first told me she was going to write a book, I had no idea how much of her story would be my story. Linda Lee has always had the ability to captivate an audience—either singing or speaking. Then I found myself captivated by *Believe God for Something Big*. Certainly I am a bit biased—since she is my firstborn child.

When Linda Lee was an infant, I laid her on a table in front of the pulpit while I preached. This must have indelibly marked her for ministry. As a preschooler, she would gather her stuffed animals and preach to them. As a teenager, one of her first songs was a jingle about how God makes her happy. As an adult, she has become a strong woman of faith and influence through her music and personal testimony.

I am so proud to be her father and to be the recipient of such honor by my daughter. My prayer for you, having read this book, is that you will personally be convinced of how merciful and faithful the Lord Jesus Christ is—and how much He loves you.

Senior Pastor David L. White

Printed in the United States
By Bookmasters